The Think Book

"385 Original Quotes on an array of
topics that will Reshape Your Thinking"

- Dr. Larry D. Reid

The Dedication

This book of Original Quotes is literally my thoughts in ink, "the true shape of my head", concerning an array of topics. This work is dedicated to all the people that made mistakes and shared them with me and to my personal hodgepodge of influential leaders, friends, enemies and troublemakers. This motley composition yielded the good and the bad along with piercing pressures, excruciating life lessons, all mixed with joyful bliss. It was in those changing times, that these wisdoms and divine thoughts were born. In those seasons I gave myself to the Holy Spirit, the Word of God, prayer and much meditation. I hope that you enjoy what you read and your thinking impacted forever.

Special Thanks

I am grateful to the other great minds who contributed to the colorful collage that I am inside. You have inspired me. Your inspiration has prompted me to compile this "manuscript of my innards" for others to read and glean from, as I have gleaned from your life. I pray that the mind, heart, and spirit of those that read be changed and charged by the barrage of inspiration that will permeate and pierce them through as they read.

My Inspirers

The Holy Spirit
The Bible
Mike Murdock
Linwood Stevenson
Myles Monroe
Elijah Forte
Odell Forte
Tedaro Reid Sr.
Ethelene Reid
Ida B. Fleming
Bernard Jordan
Joyce Meyers
Douglas Fleming
Frank Summerfield
John Eckhardt
I. V. Hilliard

TABLE OF CONTENTS

General Quotes

1. The true devil is ignorance. Knowledge that brings wisdom is God.

2. Ignorance is the irritation of the sensible.

3. All seeds have weeds, and among weeds are choking seeds.

4. There is no evil in anyone, only the lack of awareness of God. Ignorance is the greatest evil known to man.

5. If it's not challenging, it's not God.

6. When you're doing a bad job or making a mess of your life, and no one points it out to you, that means, they've given up on you and the possibility of you ever changing.

7. If there's a dysfunction, then there's an invading system that is causing impairment. The first step in clearing the matter is naming or identifying the invading system.

8. Among the voices in life that you will hear, and pay much attention to, your voice is most important. Hearing and knowing your own voice gives you identity and self awareness, which is the prerequisite of knowing all things, even God.

9. Holiness is not a performance but rather a lifelong pursuit.

10. People have God and they don't even know it. There is no way you could've made it through certain things in life except you're knitted and tied to God already. He is the sustaining agent through tragedy. Thy spirit sustains thee through all tragedy.

11. At the root of the disease of addiction is selfishness and self-centeredness.

12. Sin burns deep. Sin residing within for a considerable length of time, reconstructs your innards, making you privy to unclean spirits. Even after the spirits leave, your spiritual self, emotional self, thought patterns and etcetera are all in disarray. It can mean years of repair after the spirits are banished.

13. When things die or are brought to a close, know that God is screaming shift.

14. Adversity is your friend, that's why it is called add-versity. No matter what it is, you gain from it all. Adversity weathered correctly adds versatility, flexibility, responsibility, and capability.

15. Alone is one of those places that will be whatever you make it. You can make it a place of blessing or your mental demise.

16. Anything not under control (order or restraint) Satan freely patrols.

17. There are more responsibilities in freedom than there are in bondage. The difference is, in freedom there are consequential responsibilities. In bondage there are demanding obligations. Bondage limits choice while freedom liberates us to choose. The responsibility of freedom is managing more things.

18. All fire is hot and all fire burns, but the hottest fire of them all is backfire.

19. When in doubt, don't! Doubt doesn't mean never, but it definitely means not right now under these conditions. Don't move an inch when there is doubt or you will slowly sink into sightless mindlessness.

20. Most are in need of change and then better. Better has been the bread of bastards. Better doesn't belong to brainless, lazy bastards who are allergic to adaptation and reformation. Better rightfully belongs to changed persons who face the pressures of progression, and the arduousness of re-adjustment for the cause of advancement.

21. The longer the stronger. Staying in a strong place a long time is the key to life change.

22. There is a wealth of wisdom to be gained in weakness. Many never find her because of their masculine mentality and unwillingness to admit weakness. The lessons learned in weakness will yield strength for success.

23. Witchcraft is to control someone by domination, intimidation, manipulation, as well as adoration, validation, and compensation.

24. One of the first stages of healing is hurt. It follows exposure.

25. Are you ignoring me? I know you can hear me! I am the sickening sound of sameness. I am sent by God to provoke new movement. Stagnation sickens the soul and castrates your creativity. Give mind to the nagging noise of sameness, which is your alarm. Move quickly before your cycle goes silent and you fall "sound asleep".

26. The second choice that anyone makes is the intended remedy of a first choice gone bad.

27. Few people are fake and oblivious to it. Believe me. They are fake, and they know it. Facades are chosen over and over before they become an unconscious habitual way of living.

28. One of the smartest people you can ever listen to is the one that's been the dumbest.

29. Where there is darkness there is light. They exist side by side independent of each other. If you're in darkness push through unto its end, for there's an eye blinding bright side.

30. The person that's insecure is likely to be given to the temptation to control others. In an effort to give to themselves the security that they need, they secure all things dear to them as a security guard would secure precious merchandise.

31. Some people tend to see in others what they don't see in themselves. Who are they? They are the *helpselfdicapped*. They claim to have sensitive noses and smell everything except their own stink. Their wisdom only works for others. Having their eyes turned inside out so that they can see inside of themselves, is the gift that we all want to give to them. They are handicapped. They are *helpselfdicapped*.

32. Upon entering someone, demons propagate dysfunction. Dysfunction itself is a divine draw for demons, from the least of them to the greatest of them.

33. Most of us try to get past things instead of grow past things. Throwing things away, instead of growing things away profits little in comparison.

34. Cycles can only occur when participating variables refuse to change.

35. There is a well in hell. From that well in your hell, you *draw* the waters of wisdom, the treasures of treachery, the success that sabotage creates, and exceptionality. Your hell may seem unjust, but it's truly a radically ridiculous reservoir uniquely designed for your *drawing pleasure*.

36. Maturity is time and timing. Maturity is to take your time and maturity happens over time. Maturity is time and timing.

37. If you aren't as open as possible, then you're closed to what is possible.

38. Different to us means learning for us.

39. In the American culture it seems that dumb is the new smart, out of order is the new order, waiting patiently is idle, and mass consciousness is the accepted consciousness. If you're going to make your own mark, you must defy the accepted system and standard, and journey against the grain full throttle non-stop, to make a difference and be different. Redefine it all.

40. What is necessary is never unwise.

41. As it relates to internal wars, sometimes going to bed early is half the battle.

What Are You Thinking Now?

_____
_____
_____
_____
_____
_____
_____
_____
_____
_____
_____
_____
_____
_____
_____
_____
_____
_____
_____
_____
_____
_____
_____
_____
_____
_____
_____
_____
_____
_____

Quotes about You And for You

1. When your product precedes you, then prosperity is your prediction, fame is the fruition, and wealth will be your permanent condition.

2. It is easier to deprive yourself than it is to discipline yourself. A person that deprives himself is isolated from experience while he that is disciplined, manages all things he experience.

3. Evil is to live your life backwards.
   [E V I L / L I V E]

4. When what you know is wrong, starts to feel right and then subsequently is believed to be right, there is no more Light. All Light has been removed from you and the self rules as Lord.

5. Don't go blindly forward unaware. If you must handle snakes then be immune to venom. Awareness is your anti-venom.

6. The person who chooses heaven or hell is stronger than the person torn between the two.

7. The truth is this, you love the lie! You don't want to hear the truth, or know the truth. You'd rather hear more of what you like to hear. You shouldn't continue this way. If it hurts, tell yourself the truth. Be straight up! The best thing you'll ever hear is the last thing you'll want to hear - the truth.

8. Your form is not your reality, but your reality is your form.

9. You can't let go of what you haven't embraced. You must own up to your ugly truths and fully embrace them, and from that place of truth, progression can be made.

10. Only after the smoke clears, can you really see what's on fire and burning. The smoke inhibiting your vision and stirring panic and shock in your emotions will cause you to waste water on something that isn't on fire or burning.

11. Holding on to the past is the adolescence in many adults, the childishness of men, and the Achilles Heel of champions. Choose maturity and face the past, fumble with it if you must, and then flee it, let it go, and follow your future's fruition.

12. God will never ask you to do anything you can do in your own strength, but remember your spirit can do anything.

13. My original state is immaterial. I am spirit. I am known in the spirit world in this state, and that is my original state. God knows me in this nonmaterial state. My original self.

14. My being is spirit, not human.

15. You thicken despair, when yourself to others, you compare.

16. You aren't what you do, but you are or will be what you continually do.

17. You can't dismiss chaos without bringing order.

18. There are two seeds in you. The seed of God, which grows a tree, and the seed of the flesh, which grows weed. Sometimes the only way to manage the weed is to continue to allow your tree roots to grow deep as the weeds grow high. Some weeds are to be removed while some are to be managed by your God-ness.

19. When you're not doing what God has said to you, then you're aiming to undo all that He has said about you.

20. Ego is to Exclude **God's Omniscience**. How big is yours?

21. Deception is the result of compromise. Keep your standards and you'll keep your discerning eye.

22. There is a place in each of us we must master, and if you mention that place it will scare others. But if you conquer that place it will yield a blessing you can't believe, which will yield the praise of others.

23. A lack of awareness throws the accuracy of all information one receives into an unrealized and even distorted state.

24. A person's perspective comes from their inner self. So if there is a warp in me then there is a warp in what I see.

25. You are or will become your habits.

26. Find your flaw and deal with it! What you don't fix will flower.

27. Don't encumber your future successes by getting in right now messes.

28. Just because they don't know your worth, doesn't mean you have none. Go where your talents are realized and your gifts are celebrated. Don't be dumb-ed down. You are greatness hidden for an appointed time!

29. There's a strategy to everything. Your mistakes and successes are all part of a strategy that God over watches to show you, teach you, develop you, and grow you.

30. A liar never purpose in their heart to tell the truth. So when they decide to tell the truth, question them, listen to them carefully, and you will discover the real truth unbeknownst to them. Make sure you draw your conclusions from what is revealed thereby, not from what was spilled from their world of fantasy, error, and lies, in their selfish effort to tell the truth.

31. When people stop pushing you to do better, that means they have given up on you ever being sane enough to change. So if you're being pushed to look in the mirror, it is best for you to look while you still have eyes.

32. You may ask yourself why is it that whenever I do good, evil is always there? It's there to keep you in the harmony of contradiction which is the crucible of innovation and invention. Managing the in-between keeps you in a yielding balance.

33. Whatever you see when you close your eyes is a conglomerate of who you are or who you will become. If you see nothing then you've yet to find yourself, your interests, or your motivations.

34. There is no one growing and developing at the same rate and speed you are. We are uniquely evolving.

35. Torn between two ideas are you? Then follow the idea that leads to freedom. The believer's freedom has God and God-things at its center.

36. When it's offered to you harmlessly free, you'll ultimately pay much more than what you'd be willing to pay otherwise. In such instances harmless is harmful and careful isn't careful enough.

37. In order to fix dysfunction, you must stop functioning. You cannot continue to behave dysfunctionally and expect repair.

38. When spiritual progression seems to be hard work over time to obtain skill normalcy, you are striving for spirituality by the flesh. Spirituality only requires dying unto God. A sacred surrender.

39. It's only good to live in your head when your head is healthy. Otherwise those of us on the outside could be unsuspecting pawns for your fanatical, sadistic, deviant, or twisted inner reality - a crazy mind movie starring anyone or me!

40. Those of you that lord your bellies shall rule as kings.

41. Take the extra out of extraordinary by making unusually remarkable conventional.

42. Know your encourager. Those that say "I am proud of you" could actually testify of a consciousness they've had concerning you which was, disbelief in your ability to change behavior, or accomplish a goal. They could have doubted you at some point. Those that say nothing are those who haven't discerned your worth, neither are they conscious of your purpose. Those that say "I knew you could, I knew you would be," are those who have always

believed in you, whether you were up
or down, or in or out at the time.

43. A lot of times the last person to know
the real truth about you is you. We must
be more conscious of ourselves.

44. Sometimes struggling to fit into what
isn't for you is the first step in finding
your authentic self.

45. We're all right from our own view, so
it's wise to see from the view of a friend,
a teacher, and even an enemy for a
composite view of yourself - which is
more than likely who you are
comprehensively and your most true
self. Choose to be your best self.

46. The anointing and arrogance are often
foe-twins liken unto the flesh and the
spirit, Esau and Jacob, and good and
evil. Make one serve the other!

47. If there's an array of people that are
saying the same thing about you after
dealing with you - there is truth to it.

48. If you're not doing all that you can do
now, you won't do all of what's required
of you then.

49. How you do when you're small is how you'll do when you're big.

50. If you aren't clear about your purpose and who God has created you to be, most likely you're copying someone. Seek your original.

51. Proper character over time will change your scarred reputation.

52. You're going around the same mountain a new way with new people. The result shall be the same because you aren't new. You're the same. Change *you* into new, and so will *same*.

53. The probability of bad getting worse is higher than the likelihood of change for the better - especially when you haven't adopted new patterns.

54. Think more, and you'll sin less.

55. Change feels like what you've never done before. It feels strange, but it's the change you're seeking.

56. Everyone at some point must deal with the perils of outer appearance. Accepting what you can't change instantly and loving it properly is a journey.

What Are You Thinking Now?

_____
_____
_____
_____
_____
_____
_____
_____
_____
_____
_____
_____
_____
_____
_____
_____
_____
_____
_____
_____
_____
_____
_____
_____
_____
_____
_____
_____
_____

Quotes about Feelings, Energies and Emotions

1. Sin isn't smart, it's emotional. Irrational thinking always yields a stupid mistake or a mindless move.

2. Choose elevation over emotions and principle over passions.

3. The negative are nag-ative; always nagging about something. Where there is nag-ativity there is negativity.

4. Not even the best actor can mime the love factor. It's the greatest energy there is. It's the energy from which other energies, that are essential for the good-life experience, flow out of.

5. Feeling better doesn't mean better at all. It's just a feeling. Changing things inwardly (which eventually manifests outwardly) is truly better.

6. Fear believes the fact of the matter, not the Truth of it. Do not fear.

7. You're great at creating the "filled feeling". What if the truth is that what you are choosing to be filled with isn't real? What if it's all one elaborate fantasy and isn't as you assume? What if it's actually harmful for you and not good, as it seems? Don't trust the "filled feeling". Don't let the "filled feeling" gauge your actions and decisions.

8. A man is never the cause of your displeasure - it's the energies that come through that man.

9. You should lust for them because you love them. You shouldn't love as a result of your lust after them. That really isn't love at all.

10. With your vibration, or faithfully charging positive energy, you can charge people and things (as we do in ordination, dedications, consecrating of oils, cloths, and water).

11. Your soul's vibration, awareness and condition, downloads in the things you handle or possess. Your consciousness gets recorded into it. Watch whose clothes you wear, and whose things you handle.

12. If your adverse thoughts, feelings, and emotions are left unattended, they will damage you, your environment, and those that live in it. Your environment, and others, will suffer greatly, but you will suffer more. Those damaging emotions will bring what you fear the most - near and close. The realm you think in, you will live in.

13. Traumas, rejection, neglect, and such, cause an earthquake in the soul. This splitting or break that happens in a person can be described as a fracture. Fractures cause us to be dysfunctional emotionally, socially and spiritually. This will affect every relationship in our life beginning with the relationship we have with ourselves. While it is true that the remedy to every fracture we suffer is God, remedy and repair begins with us looking within ourselves, with the power and strength that we have, and initiate repair.

14. An open and unhealed wound will distort and possibly negate the truth of it all.

15. The flesh will follow the feeling. Manage your feelings and rule your behavior.

16. So you think what you are dealing with is getting old? Well have you forgotten that you are too? Save thyself! Don't trip over what you are dealing with any longer. Don't waste your energy and time away.

17. The day you realize that it has become your crack, is the day you must pull back.

18. The most pure and precious kind of encouragement, is energy conjured from within. Only you can summons it. It's inspiration from within. The encouragement and inspiration that comes from others is great but it is momentary, and cannot be willed by you. Conjure your inner powers of encouragement, and feed from them at will.

19. Our desire directs us most of the time, not our knowledge. When knowledge becomes your compass, your destination is limitless continual success in all areas of your life wisdom bred.

20. Loneliness and boredom cause emotional pain that longs desperately to be eased. Don't allow this desperation to move you to mindless consumption.

21. Unprocessed pain will make you insane.

22. Never allow yourself to grow and progress in evil. What you haven't done or experienced on your "list of pleasurable perversions undone" let them go. Let the undone go out of your want. Disentangle your desire, and allow the power of God to undo all the things you have done.

23. Discipline and restraint are pillars of strength, and not strenuous overbearing control, when it's an energy *you* are producing from within.

24. Sometimes faithfulness to His Will has its greatest yield when His Will isn't what you feel.

25. Finding peace within is the key to winning the war without.

26. Patience is your power and strength, as change happens as a process instead of an event.

27. The person, who has a void, seeks for the voice on the outside of themselves to "fill them up". Consequently, whatever or whoever fills them up, is lord over them.

28. Intentional or not intentional - hurt still hurts. Direct and on purpose or by default and as the result of - hurt still hurts. Wholly healing from hurt is hard, but it never leaves a scar. Only God can heal you whole and scar-less.

29. The mission of all energy toward us is summated in the following: energize, mentalize, and materialize. Energy wants voice, and desires form. You exercise control over what materializes, through managed energized-mentalization. Only allow the energy you want formed.

30. Those who are suppressing are depressing. They keep themselves from living their lives free. When things are held inside, those things become firmly rooted and diseases form. One of the cures for those who are suppressing and depressing is expressing.

31. In God there is no yesterday or tomorrow. God operates in the eternal now. We are locked into time because of our thinking. Let us think as God thinks so that when He speaks, it can be.

32. Feelings often exist void of hard evidence or real facts about what is true. No matter how intense, remember they're just feelings.

33. A fracture can be ignored, but it will demand your attention in the near future, severely inopportune.

34. Happiness is an immaterial force that you conjure from the inside. Drink your fill. The hangover is joy.

35. If you feel strong about it, you're not likely to see what's wrong about it.

36. Love is the spirit of our faith.

What Are You Thinking Now?

_____
_____
_____
_____
_____
_____
_____
_____
_____
_____
_____
_____
_____
_____
_____
_____
_____
_____
_____
_____
_____
_____
_____
_____
_____
_____
_____
_____

Quotes about Your Mind's Thoughts And Thinking

1. The idle mind is the illness of idiots.

2. God wants your mind to change. It must
    be transformed, it must be renewed, and
    it must be reborn.

3. Your mind experience is your God
    experience.

4. An insatiable desire to be fulfilled will
    yield preposterous thinking, which is
    the seed of fantasy. Blinded by strong
    desire, decisions are made that can
    change your life forever and cost you
    the invaluable. Sin is the result of
    illogical thinking. Irrational thinking
    itself is sin.

5. Quietness isn't quietness at all. It's the
    only time you can hear everything as it
    is.

6. Thankfulness is to have thoughts full of
    thanks. Thankfulness is think-fullness. If
    you aren't think-full as you praise, you
    aren't thankful in your praise. Your
    thoughts determine your praise. So a
    breach in thankful thoughts is also a
    breach in your praise.

7. Your meditation affects your worship
    and your belief system.

8. A carnal mind deciphering spiritual things will ultimately yield an antichrist mindset structured by the spirit of religion, rebellion, apostasy, and error.

9. Whatever I think about will come about.

10. Resist the devil and fight the good fight of faith. What you fight tends to draw your focus, and what you focus on expands. Fight the way God instructs. Focus on your faithful fight, not the devil.

11. I don't think I am God, God thinks He is me, for in this earth I am He. I must think as He thinks. I must daily empty God of all His thoughts and let Him live His wants, desires and purposes through me.

12. A person's home will house their consciousness and level of thinking. My mind is my house.

13. If God isn't in your mouth, then He can't be in your mind (Joshua 1:8). If God isn't in your mind, your mouth will utter Godless words.

14. Whatever we are thinking about, we're thanking about. What are you exalting? What are you praising?

15. Fuel your positive thoughts, affirmations, and visualizations with feelings. Strong desire and passion is the divinity of your soul and the energy offering for your faith. Mesh your creative power with God's ultimate power and see things created.

16. Mind the things of the Spirit and inspire yourself. Mind the things of the flesh and erode yourself.

17. You are a creator. Whether you are conscious of it or not, you are a creator. What kind of life are you creating for yourself and those around you? You are thinking it all up!

18. God communicates with us through our thoughts. What is on your mind? Is it a thought that welcomes other thoughts from the Spirit?

19. When will it happen? When will I have the thing that I've been thinking on? When will it manifest? Well it depends on your consciousness, your awareness, your vibratory energy offering and your physical preparedness.

20. God said be fruitful as those with dominion and multiply. Your thoughts are the father of your future. All of your things are the children of your consciousness. How many children do you have? What kind of children are you having?

21. Mass consciousness is never ready for revelatory truth. Only a remnant is ready for the true reveal.

22. Every thought is a seed that will produce a harvest for me.

23. You will think, speak and act at the corresponding level of Word you take in daily.

24. When our thinking changes, we will see God move faster. He desires to move instantaneously. God exists in the eternal now. He desires to operate in the eternal now. He speaks and it is so. Our fractured thinking demands God's gift of time. God uses time that man can develop and grow into himself.

25. Our thoughts, words, and deeds strengthen angels. If it is a thought, word, or deed of the flesh it strengthens demons. A thought, word, or deed of the Spirit strengthens the Angels of God.

26. The mind must rule the belly else the belly will rule the mind. The mind in my belly must be ruled by the mind of God that is in me.

27. In order to effectively affect the lives of others, our consciousness must extend beyond the self. At that point, we can discern the consciousness of others and advance their thinking and overall thought pattern. Are you well enough for this arduous task?

28. One thoughtless action can seed your life for a horrid harvest. Think things through, and change what comes to you.

29. Uncertainty is in fact certainty. It is a state of awareness. Awareness itself is therapeutic to our existence, and curative in nature.

30. From the time you first thought, "It doesn't make sense", know that you've been dumb ever since.

31. There is power in conformation but *the power* exists in transformation. A transformed mind is a transformed life.

32. Mainstream is the thought, word, and behavior patterns that are accepted among the masses and is subliminally suggested to us all, all of the time. Make sure your thoughts are your own.

What Are You Thinking Now?

Quotes about Relationships, Alliances and Associations

1. We should seek to walk with those that are pregnant with what we are pregnant with.

2. Because you crossed the lines - lines must be redrawn that are much bolder, more evident, and apparent. If you don't like living life restrained as such, then never cross the lines! Abiding by those innately preset parameters in relationship matters, should be a part of your humanity.

3. The drive to fellowship with others at a time when God is saying to be alone is your flesh and your demon, trying to feed in an effort to cause deviation or abortion in your life.

4. Whenever you have to tell someone how to love you (especially repeatedly), it is time to love yourself differently.

5. Relationship first and then discipleship. When discipleship isn't preceded by relationship, the truth you share is more likely to be rebelled against.

6. When you say that you love someone or are in love with someone, remember that these emphatic declarative statements are predicated upon your present state of awareness and experience. You may look back two years from now in realization and say, "I didn't love that person, neither was I ever in love with them."

7. Categorize people by their capacity so that you won't be sorry, and they won't be either. It is stressful on their part trying to portray volume that they truly don't own or hold. You must do what will appear to others as being impersonal, and compartmentalize those that are in your life. The wrong people, in the wrong place, at the wrong time will immobilize you and cost you prosperity.

8. Whoever sees your worth is the person that will do nothing but build you, support you, and inspire you to be the best you. Anyone who stifles or trifles who you are or can become is your enemy. God only allows them there for a season - awaiting you to outgrow them.

9. If a person doesn't stay in your life of their own free will, they do not play a part in the fulfillment of your destiny and most likely didn't come from God.

10. Fraternizing at your church or on your job is mindless! If it goes bad then you're tempted to remove yourself from one of them, and most likely you will. Who can live without their income? Who can live without their spiritual nexus? Make wise relationship choices and don't encumber your life.

11. Who you're around will determine your ground, and your ground determines what will grow up for you.

12. Anyone who cannot give you what you need is sent by hell to distract you and ultimately drain and derail you.

13. As a people we must shift from the mindset of me to *us*. If you want to be rich, you must never act without considering the *us* factor. The rich serve more people than the poor. Serve more and you'll not be poor. I call this the McDonald's Concept (billions served).

14. Is it possible for someone to be my friend, supporter, teammate, colleague, associate and helper, but in a relationship with my enemy, challenger, component, combatant, rival and antagonist? I think not. They're either in agreement with my enemy or me - they're faking it with one of us.

15. Distraction is the enemy. You must pay attention, which is focused persistence, upon God's Good Will. *You must release those that break focus*, because they waste energy and cause you to lose focus. In the realm of thought, attention and focus is currency that you must have to pay to those things that you want to manifest.

16. When you look inward, you should see a person you would want to be with forever. If that is not the case, then wait a while before you bring someone into your life.

17. If you aren't strengthened by being with a person, then cut them off. If you don't, you're signing up for the pain, so don't speak again of your strain.

18. Leaders rarely have friends. Leaders are careful not to throw their emotions behind anyone in an absolute way, because if it doesn't produce properly, the forward moving leader must face the paralyzing painful risk of cutting it off. This is the Law of Separation within the kingdom for the King, and those in His court.

19. Those around you reveal you.

20. Almost always, a man is necessary for anything from God to pass to you.

21. Make sure that the person in your ear isn't an antagonist to the authority in your life. They will cause strife and separation between you and that necessary authority.

22. Whatever is in your ear will manifest in your year. Who is in your ear?

23. I can only come to myself. Discern the type of people, places, and things you are attracted to. They are you!

24. When someone hasn't found the intimacy, wholeness, and happiness that only God gives in perfection, anything or anyone that brings them any form of happiness or satisfaction can easily become their idol, new bondage, or new addiction. That thing or person is their painkiller.

25. If you really love the Lord, He will remove all props and void fillers without your permission. This may cost you a relationship or many relationships.

26. Zero in on people's strength and you will protect yourself from suspicion and from criticizing of others.

27. Liberate yourself from the ignorance of those around you who are mindlessly handling your greatness. It's time for you to skillfully change your environment and pepper in people who are conscious of your worth and celebrate it.

28. Be careful of the spirit of control. At times the controller cloaks the evil power they have over you in validation and verification. After you're feeling approved, accomplished and needed, they slowly introduce your obligations for the purposes of regulation. This isn't your reasonable service! You're being manipulated by a wicked spirit of control.

29. There is nothing wrong with having to work on your relationship, but never try to work on your love. True love exists in authentic perfection and grows bright (as a love light) as your relationship skills strengthen.

30. Reconciliation is an art that only Jesus has perfected and many men have neglected. Reconciliation can only happen after two persons have humbly opened themselves to its possibilities, and then seek to solve their inner puzzles, struggles and difficulties. Radical Reconciliation.

31. Two healthy mature people create one whole of the same.

32. The relationship you have with yourself, others and God grow at the same speed.

33. Neither your ugly nor your pretty are original, no matter how extraordinary people make you feel that it is. Yes, you heard me right. There is someone out there that matches your ugliness and your prettiness. Like attracts like, so if you don't like what you have attracted, then check your areas of ugliness and prettiness. There's a match out there for everyone.

34. No true and real covenant can faithfully exist in feelings alone. True and real covenants faithfully exist in action provoking knowledge and awareness that constitutes commitment.

35. They really aren't the love of your life, they are the love of your lie.

36. The void place in you is aching and wanting that warm filled feeling. Be careful what you put in the void, for it will spread and fill you, and become the source of your satisfaction.

37. The reality of duality is individuality.

38. Never let nothing be said. When nothing is said, then anything and everything is being thought and possibly believed, by the one you should be communicating to.

39. Love is given, expressed, and possessed at the level of knowledge one possesses. You can gauge love levels by assessing the knowing level. Who really knows you, is who really loves you. You may love what you know about me, but what you know about me is only what I show about me. To know me is to love me.

40. Addicts will substitute their drug or addiction of choice with a relationship. Normally the two are tied together and part of each other. The addict will find a mate to match them in their addiction. If the addict wants change they will need to separate from their drug or addiction of choice and most likely the person or people they have been connected with.

41. When someone says that they need you to help them, stop and see where they are helping themselves before you become their prop, crutch or even idol.

42. If you've just met them and within the first few conversations they start telling you sensitive information concerning them or someone else, you should proceed with caution, if at all.

43. If you hear a rumor and you have a relationship with any of the parties of the rumor, it's now your concern too!

44. If you hear a rumor from someone and you know the person that's being discussed, refute the rumor and then go to the person being discussed to talk to him or her for yourself, bearing no names.

45. Unity among the few is the might that smites the many.

46. Choosing a mate is actually match-making your inner core self with someone else's.

47. Before you sex - sync! Sexual activities should follow in depth inquiry. Do you share the same core values, goals, or beliefs? Go beyond the skin my friends. Sync before sex! You may find that you only like the skin that they're in.

48. Love obsession makes people blind to red flags. This obsession can cause bad choices that alter lives forever.

49. If you're in love with someone that's crazy, then you're stupid by selection. Be silent about your dilemma and accept the responsibility of selection.

50. It's good to be transparent for many
    reasons; however, it's wise to be
    transparent only with those you should
    be transparent with. Even then it should
    be done tactfully, and with carefulness.

What Are You Thinking Now?

_____

_____

_____

_____

_____

_____

_____

_____

_____

_____

_____

_____

_____

_____

_____

_____

_____

_____

_____

_____

_____

_____

_____

_____

_____

_____

_____

_____

_____

_____

_____

Quotes about the Prophet, The Prophetic And Music

1. Pleading promises and reciting prophecies while violating principles will never produce God-things.

2. If I am given to idols, I-dull my spirit to the things of God. I lose ear to Him.

3. There is the word of the prophet and then there is the Word of the Lord. The word of the prophet most times is the Word of the Lord.

4. As a prophet, what you don't see, the Lord has hid from you. He hides it so that you can experience it in a way you wouldn't have chosen for yourself to experience it, neither the way the person you are prophesying to would have chosen for themselves to experience it. This is the part the prophet will not know in the prophetic flow.

5. The prophet's sight is sometimes like an eagle hovering overhead. The prophet shouldn't hover where his sight hasn't been honored. When one honors with a seed, you have permission to see for them. This doesn't imply that a prophet can only see for those who sow financially.

6. The song you sing will be an affirmation of what you have experienced, are experiencing, or will experience. Be sure to sing songs that are prophetic of where God says you are going. Sing about, what you dream about.

7. Prophets have an ability to create conditions with the Word of the Lord.

8. One of the key factors in determining if we have heard the voice of God within ourselves, and not a spirit sent from Satan to deceive us is honesty. If in our heart we are honest and true to ourselves, others, and God, we will always hear His voice. Everyone that is of the truth hears His voice (John 18:37 KJV). He who is of God will hear His words (John 8:47 KJV).

9. In times of transition men and women of God can be bombarded by spiritual impressions and unctions that can provoke events, situations, projects, moves, and even purchases that are not the Will of God for their lives or are premature for their lives. When we make decisions based on those spiritual impressions that come to us during these transitional seasons and assign their validity to the sovereign One, we commit spiritual forgery.

10. All dreamers, prophetics, prophets, seers and sensors, hear this, "God is a mirror!

11. Hearing God isn't simply a deciphering of His words. It's discerning the intent of His Will. Sons hear their father's heart. It's those unspoken words that only they can hear.

12. I know we do well to listen to the words of God through a messenger of God, but what I have learned recently is that we should pay even closer attention to the words that God speaks through us. We aren't without direction as it seems, neither are we as oblivious to His plans for us, as we think. Your much needed directive is sitting within you, waiting to be discovered by your awareness.

13. When someone inquires of a prophet it is important that the prophet discerns if the person wants to have their pains soothed by the word of good that may flow out of the prophets mouth, or if they want to hear truth. The truth is whatever is on God's mind now concerning them.

14. Your song, prayer, praise, and your worship are all done from the same place. Your level in the prophetic will flow from that same place.

15. Want to know the state of mind a person has? Look at their music collection. Bad music equals bad mind. Bad music (or what I call low music) sings to the emotions only and not the mind.

16. Walk faithfully in what God has spoken prophetically, until He speaks again.

17. There are repercussions for not doing faithfully what God has spoken prophetically, and there are repercussions for doing by faith what God hasn't spoken prophetically.

18. My giftedness runs quick, placing itself ahead of my goodness, as I am in steady pursuit of godliness. I should give more attention to my pursuit, than my sprinting gifts.

19. The prophetic realm is the realm within the Kingdom of God where God makes known the unknown. All of what is made known by God in this realm serves the kingdom purpose of yielding

men and women who live lives that
display Christ.

20. The prophet should master the realm of
the emotions, music and words. One of
these three will be that prophet's most
vital tool in expressing the mood and
mode of God to the hearer.

21. Conversations are concoctions and
brews. The things you talk about are
prophetic potions that bring about. Be
sure to brew conversations that
correspond with what you want to
embody.

22. A false prophet is indeed a prophet,
therefore not all prophets are prophets
of God.

23. God's prophets must do more than
operate in their psychic ability. They
must turn man's heart from mammon
unto God.

24. Improper leaders, yield improper
people. When leaders are un-repented,
they're the responsibility of God's
prophet, not the people.

What Are You Thinking Now?

_____
_____
_____
_____
_____
_____
_____
_____
_____
_____
_____
_____
_____
_____
_____
_____
_____
_____
_____
_____
_____
_____
_____
_____
_____
_____
_____
_____
_____

Quotes about Man's Faith, Money, and his Things

1. Money without prosperity of soul is a mask to many miseries. Money that doesn't reflect my soul's health, mask many truths concerning me.

2. You must watch money all the time. Money moves. It is a current (currency). Something is always happening with it even when you're not aware or looking. Pay attention before it moves away from you, and out of the place you left it last.

3. Faith is an assuredness that what you're hoping for, is manifesting. What I am sure of will manifest right before my eyes.

4. Money is recyclable and is a moving current (currency). When we put it where it's lawful as stewards (i.e. debts and also charitable giving) it continues its flow to and through us. As we become better stewards, then the flow grows. Don't stop your flow. Cause your money to grow.

5. You must be honest about money to yourself, others, and God. Dishonesty stops the flow of God to and through you.

6. Kingdom people don't have jobs (i.e. **J**ust **O**ver **B**roke). Kingdom people are assigned to companies that will empower them to give and fund God's agenda in the earth. Kingdom people do not work jobs for a check as others do. They are assigned to companies. On this wise, kingdom people have assignments (**A**postolic **S**uccess **S**hall be **I**ssued **G**reatly **N**ow that **M**y **E**nergy is **N**o longer **T**ied to a check).

7. Most yearn before they learn, and as a result, they never earn. All that's put in their hand goes out due to their lust-filled yearning.

8. Energy wasted is time wasted. He who wastes time will waste more in money.

9. The worse thing about having no money isn't the absence of money; it's the absence of relationship with money. The carefulness that is tied to money management is absent. When the relationship with money is absent, your management skills aren't being utilized. Getting money, having money, keeping money and the issuing out of money, is a masterful experience that develops stewardship. Refuse to live without the money experience.

10. The more often you get paid, the more likely you are to waste money.

11. Instead of *not* saving at all, start saving small.

12. Passion Purchasing is one of the greatest enemies of having the finances that you will need.

13. If you can't manage wisely the money you have, you are not mature enough for the options that more money will bring. More money means more responsibility, wisdom, and self-control you'll need to have in to manage more options.

What Are You Thinking Now?

_____

_____

_____

_____

_____

_____

_____

_____

_____

_____

_____

_____

_____

_____

_____

_____

_____

_____

_____

_____

_____

_____

_____

_____

_____

_____

_____

_____

Quotes about the Giver
And Giving

1. The heart regulates the hands, and everything put in them.

2. Giving starts beyond the ten percent (the tithe). The tithe opens or accesses the windows of heaven, and the offering determines what these windows yield. If the tithe belongs to God and is the Lord's, then the true beginning of giving to God is the offering.

3. You should honor the Lord with the first fruit of all your increase. For every *thing* God gives to you, a offering should be given to honor the Lord for that *thing*.

4. Sow, sow, sow, and you will know, grow and show.

5. Among other things, your vow is your spiritual identification card to God.

6. God sees the seed, as well as the need (maybe even before He sees the need). Eliminate your needs by sowing seeds. You can give yourself out of one place and into a better place.

7. To be available to God is to be available to others. Give yourself to either and you're giving to them both.

8. The offering must be from a willing heart. It must be a sacrifice and given cheerfully. Remember to expect any return from God. Return takes many forms. When you give, you receive.

9. When I give to someone I am giving what I possess and what I have, no matter how futile. If I believe I have nothing, then that's truly what I am giving and there will be no real return.

10. Only lend, give, or help those that are doing wisely with what they have.

11. The financial priority of the believer is 1. Give 2. Save 3. Pay Debts.

What Are You Thinking Now?

_____
_____
_____
_____
_____
_____
_____
_____
_____
_____
_____
_____
_____
_____
_____
_____
_____
_____
_____
_____
_____
_____
_____
_____
_____
_____
_____
_____
_____
_____

Quotes about God, The Church, and Kingdom Truths

1. God uses the local church to raise-up and stabilize those that have been called to kingdom service. The local church is the apostolic base that officially releases the gifts of God to the Body locally, nationally, internationally, globally and then to the world.

2. The Word, the Word, the Word! When people refuse to hear and gravitate to a certain level of consciousness and hunger for knowledge, you cannot teach the Word. You must deal in entertainment and continue in the theater of ministry, performing for pay and to pack the pew.

3. The Holy Ghost will only fall upon you in the dimension that the Word is preached, taught, or revealed to you. After the Word exposure, the corresponding dimension of the Spirit is accessed, activated, or poured upon those who heard and received (Acts 10:44, 19:2 KJV). We need weightier Word exposures so that we can access greater dimensions of the Spirit.

4. Things sent from God are sacred and assured success by structure. All sacred things need structure in order to be successful.

5. If you believe in something, then you are influenced by it, convicted by it, and convinced by it. If you are a believer in God (converted or as some say "saved") then you adhere to His ways, otherwise you're simply a liar.

6. The season of uncertainty is designed by God for your faith. It's only a season though. Seasons like this, as well as a plethora of others, make you seasoned. You must go through seasons in order to be seasoned.

7. When new revelation comes (or a new truth) then all prior knowledge is old oil. Old oil is improper when it is adhered to in a new place, or new time in the spirit.

8. Seeking God alone is not wisdom. Wisdom is seeking God first.

9. As you accomplish more in life your self-belief grows. Your self-belief is connected to your belief in God. The Church must build both of these if she desires to build men holistically.

10. The winds that blow from wounds warp the eye's sight of self, others, and God.

11. The amount of truth you receive or know, is directly connected to how much of what you think you know, you can let go.

12. The words of a book are the path you walk to get to the author's heart. This is why the Bible cannot be all there is to God. It's only the basis of all things God.

13. Fear of the unknown is not terror when it is trust in and respect for, He that knows the unknown.

14. Struggle is a reminder to us that God's way is the only way to come to our full potential.

15. Sometimes God will create a void in your life in an effort to get you to seek His mind.

16. You find the deeper things of God as you do what God wants you to do, versus not doing what He doesn't want you to do. Serving God means to serve His desire with all of your being. Serving the Lord is not a list of Can't Do's, but it is a list of Things to Do. Relationship with God is, "What can I do for you?"

17. Church people tend to demonize anyone that's a liberal thinker. This demonization causes the free thinker that would find the God that the church seeks to warp. Those free thinking radical reformers, are the breath of fresh air that the Church needs now so desperately.

18. The true order of God for your life is Truth, then you, your family, your church, and then your career. Let me explain the order. When one is connected to God for real, they seek Truth. He who seeks Truth is a seeker of God, and as a result has placed Him first. Knowing He that is Truth, makes you know you. Knowing yourself is knowing God, which not only makes your role in the family clear, but your place in the scheme of all things clear. So that explains the order: truth, then you, and then the family. Next is the local church and then your career. The local church, mirroring the family, is the hospital of the community and subsequently is your next concern. Lastly is your career. Our careers don't always serve the community in that respect, so that is why it is hypothetically last. Reorder your life!

19. At times He needs to be demystified so that you can take the practical approach in personal problem solving and decision-making.

20. Human sexuality is an actuality that "the church mentality" can never see in reality. The brutality that the laity in every locality has toward homosexuality, is the church's therapy given to these many. An uncompromising love made reality will move these souls toward everlasting remedy, and bankrupt the Enemy.

21. Religious thinking puts your thinking power in the hands of another.

22. On a broad scale, churches aren't helping the problem and modern day Christianity isn't either. They are offering intoxicating mixed drinks to men who are looking for sobriety! The wine of the world and the wine of the organized religious institution called the modern day Christian Church are intoxicating mixed drinks, while the wine of the kingdom is pure, sobering and good for the belly.

23. We need to know the truth beyond the scope of men who think they've found it. We need to hear the words of him who is seeking The Truth. Whoever is in search of Jesus Christ, finds Him when he finds the seeker, and make covenant with him.

24. Father is our highest state of awareness that many call god or God. Believers and seekers know that this awareness is found in Jesus Christ. He is the divine idea of God, who is God Himself.

25. The greatest enemy to a newfound truth is the newfound truth itself. The seeker is tempted to cease his search for more truth every time a new one is found.

26. Lies keep things simple and quiet, but the truth complicates things and disturbs everyone.

27. Heathens make great believers. They make better followers of the Lord's Truth than modern day Christians. It is hard for a heathen to be a hypocrite, after he finds Christ's Truth. However, if the heathen is given modern day Christianity he will become a hypocrite.

28. The local church is to foster a flawed family structure, but never replace it.

29. Although the root word of Christian and Christianity is Christ, be not deceived. Christ and His ways are blatantly denied among most Christians. To be a Christian and to follow Christianity in today's time is to be named among a widely accepted erroneous idea that isn't what Jesus Christ ever intended for His followers.

30. Religion and Tradition, and the restrictive bondage it imposes, are for those who aren't mature and personally disciplined enough for the liberating responsibilities that are in Jesus Christ and the Truth of His Kingdom.

31. I admonish you to look for the truth beginning with real facts. Then choose that truth, and be loosed from the lie. Go on now, get your mirror out and tell your friends to fetch theirs! It's time to find the truth of it all. You'll find God, and the truth, when you find your mirror, not a prophet.

32. True spirituality is to function as the Father would in my uniquely personalized ever-changing reality.

33. God uses you to do for others, what He has already done in you.

34. When am I penalized by God? There is a penalty that comes from God, yes there is. You would be surprised to know that this penalty doesn't come because of your wrong things. It is invoked when wrong things are not handled correctly. God penalizes those who forsake to implement His way in all things, including the wrong things, when they occur. Side Note: God's penalizations are all remedial.

35. Mysteries exist because we're not conscious. When we are, we know all things and nothing is hidden. A mystery is a hidden truth. Can God hide from Himself? He cannot! For if He could, then that would mean He's not conscious. There is nothing we cannot know about ourselves, others, and God, if we are aware and awake in Him.

36. The time continuum has been adjusted over and over. Every time man fails to shift with what God was saying, God stretches time in hopes that we can fully develop or mature into His true desire. When Adam disobeyed God, God chose to stretch and readjust time and use that

space to construct a way for man to come back to Him.

37. God swats at the proud fool, but He reaches for the one that's wisely humbled before Him.

38. Unbeknownst to most, God is learned deeper in the lows than in the highs. Your hell and your prison, you should gladly own as your wealthy place.

39. If you're distracted get ready for ruckus, because God uses those things that *have* your attention to *get* your attention. Divinely ordered chaos.

40. A wrong or dark desire doesn't supernaturally overtime change into a good or Godly desire. You have to totally, and often continually, let that desire go, and it will let you go. Only then can there be any hope of owning a true loving desire for God from the core of who you really are.

41. Those who ask today's church questions are on the brink of brilliance. They're nearing apprehension of God and His Truth.

42. At the very core of what you desire and want, is where you'll find who you truly are. It may not look anything like you thought yourself to be, hoped yourself to be, or confessed yourself to be. Whatever is at the core must be examined. If it's not Godly, let it go totally and continually. Then, love God and His ways with and from your core.

43. The weariness tied to well-doing must be weathered. Success God's way means hard work over time.

44. The smartest person you can ever listen to is a dummy. It's as if God has allowed their mindlessness for your learning.

45. What you believe about God is possibly the main thing that's keeping you from really knowing Him.

46. When He is presented and you refuse to conform, your form changes. You are twisted and apostasy is inevitable!

What Are You Thinking Now?

_____

_____

_____

_____

_____

_____

_____

_____

_____

_____

_____

_____

_____

_____

_____

_____

_____

_____

_____

_____

_____

_____

_____

_____

_____

_____

_____

_____

_____

Quotes about Prayer, Meditation and the Power of Words

1. The longer you go without praying, the harder it is to pray, and praying through effectively, is ever difficult to do. Prayerlessness, which is a spiritual comatose state, worsens over time and eventually, the spirit dies. Prayerlessness is a "silent killer". The intellectual, religious, proud, and common mind will depreciate the necessity of perfervid prayer.

2. Words are empty capsules fit for burning when they aren't in sync with your yearning.

3. Be cautious in voicing your lack or limitation. For by your words you will be catapulted, constricted, or castrated.

4. You cannot have a future in that which you aren't knowledgeable of. You must know in order to create. You must understand and know. To know is to have a correct mental view and picture, which is needed in order to create. If you know of it, then you can bring show to it. Do your part in educating yourself about what the Spirit is speaking to your mind. God will manifest, as you pray your best.

5. You don't silence the flesh with a prayer. You silence the flesh with residual prayer encounters.

6. To be in prayer is to be in the realm of the spirit **P**ushing **R**oughly **A**side **Y**our **E**vil **R**oot.

7. Walk in your authority. Instead of praying to God all the time, pray as God and speak to things.

8. Although our giftings have allowed us to stay relevant to our title, function, and position, we know deep within ourselves that we have left the quality and quantity of prayer that exalted us to where we are today. We are serving sleep. Our heart should ache for a new place of prayer, greater than where we were before, for the sake of our relationship with Father God, and not our craft.

9. The word praying describes and explains the process of the intercessor forming spirit into matter.

10. Intercessory prayer misused, is spell casting. For prayer must be Thy will be done and not my will be done.

11. Should I pray or practice? There are things that we pray about, that we should put into practice, and there are things that we are attempting to put into practice that should be prayed forth.

12. Everyone prays at the level of their awareness. As your awareness deepens, your prayer depth and impact intensifies. The power of the push and pull in your prayer stream will grow in force as your awareness of self and God broadens. You will have spiritual sharpness that will cut skillfully on your behalf and on the behalf of others.

13. One of the keys to healing your ill prayer component is awareness. Find someone to tell you the Truth about you to your face.

14. There are levels of repentance because there are levels of awareness. You repent at the level of your awareness. Re-repentance is in order and is of the Lord.

15. Prayer is thinking thoughts strongly and consistently.

16. The Spirit of God is divine assistance in the gruesome and challenging task called *you*. Pray and fix *you*.

17. What happens when you pray? Prayer travels you out of this world into spirit, then into Spirit, thus disconnecting you from your perception of reality, into God's reality. There your perspective is changed about it all. He gives you His view and His directive, and sends you back to this earthly realm with what you need to resolve issues, and to exist in your circumstances victorious. This explains one of the many happenings when you pray.

18. We must pray for others and not *on* others. When you pray with a person or situation in mind, strongly visualizing the result that you want, you are praying *on* them. You're actually preying on them verses praying for them. This will cause that person to experience lots of difficulties mentally, emotionally, and even physically. This is casting your spell. We must pray to God concerning our brother, mentioning to God what we know to be The Will of the Spirit and not our own, speaking it forth into the air around them intensely. This is praying and interceding on someone's behalf or praying for them.

Otherwise we are causing war in the lives of others instead of peace, and are witches causing forcibly our will to be done. True intercessors don't meddle in the matters of men by their will and choice, but by the direction, leading, and release of God.

19. A believer who doesn't have a life of prayer will have the same level of virtue, victory, and vision, of an unbeliever.

20. The more conscious you are in your soul and mind, the further out your vibration, or energy goes. The more you pray, bringing your conscience soul and mind before God, the more intense your vibration or energy becomes, which will affect the air around you everywhere you go.

21. Problem people and their personalities and passions, can weave a web that can prevent purpose by distracting your focus. Prayer placed in position, provokes the pulsating of Pentecostal powers that pierce pass and through the perfervid forces of problematic persons.

22. The one with the answers to what you're facing isn't the man with the money, the connections, or the rapport. The one with the answers you seek is the praying man.

23. Sadly, this is the true prayer of most. "God give me more faith to fetch things and grace to get things."

24. If there is no passion to pray, then you've never actually prayed.

25. Affirmations are a kind of prayer. Affirmative prayer stir up your energy to believe about yourself as God believes about you.

26. The pain of the altar is the greatest agony known to man.

27. Prayer, Praise, and Worship from an idolatrous adulterous prayer-less people releases strange fire that's eerily tangible to those who pray.

28. The key to effective prayer is to hone the ability to think a single thought(s) strongly, consistently, free and clear of unbelief.

29. When you teach a man how to pray, you teach him everything.

30. In this hour some will have to make the hard choice between the platform or prayer. Many times the two are at war with each other. Prayer requires time in a still waiting.

31. The uncanny ability of most unsung heroes is their exceptionally-consistent prayer life.

32. Prayer removes the lens of natural sight and causes you to see by the spirit.

33. Revelation is the knowledge that the prayer-less cannot comprehend.

What Are You Thinking Now?

Quotes about Marriage And Family

1. Parents in the home should echo the truth, that's taught in their local church. When the opposite is echo-ed in the home the children become confused, unstable, and double-minded.

2. A parent can only be what the authorities in their life have been to them. The parent will parent as they have been parented.

3. Where there is a father, there is a family. When the father is removed, makeshift families are created. The father is the beginning of the family.

4. Why do people choose to learn hard? My parents used to say, "Don't learn the hard way." Learning hard cost a lot, but learning by applying the wiser and better way is best. Obedience is better than sacrifice.

5. My community is the common unity I have with those around me or in my life circle.

6. The husband and the wife, is not mom and dad, and mom and dad, is not the husband and the wife. When this isn't remembered and revered, then the marriage and family is likely to fail. Typically when the kids leave the home, the silent demise of the relationship of husband and wife is fully realized.

7. The son becomes a man at the hands of his parents, mainly the father. God makes him a husband and his wife makes him a father.

8. The daughter becomes a woman at the hands of her parents, mainly her mother. God makes her a wife and her husband makes her a mother.

9. All married people should remember that they are not the husband or the wife. They are themselves. Individuality must be embraced prior to and along with duality.

10. Prayer is thinking thoughts strongly. When you pray with someone you think with them. It is important that families think as one often.

11. You are the largest part of your marriage and the only part that you can control.

12. Family is an energy shared among and between. Family is the intimately supportive loyal spirit of unity. Is my family really a family? Am I devoted to a tribe gone badly or an iron clan? Relation through blood, marriage, or last names alone, never fully define kinship (Matthew 12:48-50 MSG).

13. If your fat wife is going to lose weight, then the relationship cannot be fat with toxins. Outer weight means inner weights. Strive to assist and affect her psychologically until change is seen physiologically.

14. The marriage relationship is a network of bonds, ties and connections that have to be properly maintained.

15. Fathers are not named and noted greatly themselves until they are made manifest through sons. When the son manifests, the father is revealed. When the son names himself, or identifies himself, then the father is known in his fullness.

16. Within marriage, sex should be the outward manifestation of the host of positive healthy productive energies being distributed constantly between two people. When it's less than that, then it's simply sport, breeding, or a feeding frenzy.

17. If you are married to the one, that means that they are the vital part of your spiritual, emotional, and financial fulfillment, which is the basis of sexual fulfillment within the marriage relationship. If these aren't the basis of your sex life, then your marriage lacks honor and your bed is most likely defiled.

18. The marriage will not work unless the idea, option, or desire of divorce no longer exists in either spouse.

19. In a marriage relationship it is important that you allow your spouse to be who they are. If you don't like who they've become then tell them, and then pray for them. Never stop loving them. Never force them to do anything against their will, because that's really you loving yourself and not them at all.

20. Lust doesn't heed the marriage certificate. It knows no law. This lasciviousness rottens the spouse, and defiles the bed and may end it all.

What Are You Thinking Now?

_____

_____

_____

_____

_____

_____

_____

_____

_____

_____

_____

_____

_____

_____

_____

_____

_____

_____

_____

_____

_____

_____

_____

_____

_____

_____

_____

Quotes about the Vision, the Teacher And The Taught

1. When serving others isn't easy, then there's something in you unresolved.

2. Whenever and wherever God guides, He provides. We often miss the heavenly provision because we aren't in position, carrying out His vision.

3. You will only see what you have seen *in* your eye. Sight before your eyes happens after you have seen *in* your eye.

4. All birth is a rejection. It demands a separation. The baby is pushed out of the womb. Blood is drawn, the mother and the baby cry. The baby is cut away from what has fed them prior. Rejection is a form of birthing. That's why we must be healed prior to mentorship or we will push ourselves out of the birth canal, prior to the formation of vital organs. As teachers we must be careful, to not force someone out prematurely. All birth requires separation from the womb. Babies must not desire to be overgrown inside the womb due to the fear of separation.

5. Teaching others refreshes your mind and re-convicts you of those things you evicted.

6. When you receive teaching from a teacher you learn two things; you learn what they are teaching, as well as how to receive knowledge didactically. If you hope to be wise you must be able to hear and receive knowledge through teaching.

7. If he isn't humble to the Father, then he won't be humble to a father. Even if he appears to be submitted to one but not the other, know that he isn't to either.

8. When your views, opinions, and convictions are spoken in the presence of followers, it is gossip. When the same is done among leaders, you're conferencing for the purpose of counsel.

9. Being what you are saying causes others to be.

10. A minister yes, a master no. Mistakes are to be mastered. Like all men, ministers will make mistakes. Men will make mistakes, but more manfully mature than many, will that man be when he attempts to master his mistakes, and then minister to others. The marred, mistake-making minister who seeks to master his mistakes, ministers more to me than them all. A minister yes, a master, not yet.

11. The person that God uses to remove shackles from around your neck is worthy of praise and honor, but the glory belongs to God. Praise and honor that is too full becomes glory. A glorified man will place a "shackle of his own" around the neck of those that make their praise and honor too full for him. He will think himself to be a god who should be worshipped.

12. His dream is unreal to me, but it is my destiny. My dream for me must agree with my reality or my mental state is fantasy and insanity.

13. Don't preach the people of God selfish by constantly telling them about what God has for them, and their deliverance, and their breakthrough. This mentors a mind that's unable to grasp a mentality or awareness beyond itself. This type of preaching is one of the enemies to the global mentality that the local church should have.

14. Things that have been dusty a long time, dirty and unused, tend to shine better when cleaned than those already in use and appearing clean. Sometimes those we are using in leadership positions are shining as bright as they can and aren't really open to vigorous polishing anyway. Everyone wants to shine, but not everyone wants to be polished.

15. It takes more to be a teacher than it does to be an inspirer. A teacher must be an example.

16. We impart what we are, not what we say. When a person teaches they transmit their spirit.

17. Followers are careful of the power of temptation, but leaders are careful of the temptation of power.

18. You will never be as effective in changing the lives of others while you're harboring wrong motives, dishonesty, evil intent, hatred, laziness, wastefulness, and dark lust within. Bad character corrupts all your gifts. When you flow in your gift, who you are, flows as well. When you minister with your gift, you minister who you are. The singer sings their soul to you, and the preacher pours his personal inspirations all over you.

19. No matter what you think, your spiritual father just is. You do not choose them, just as you didn't choose your natural father. More than likely your spiritual father is your natural dad, or the pastor that you've submitted to for years, or the person that God sent into your life in an exceptional way, that has introduced you to God and His things in a way that nullifies all of what you knew about God.

20. The spiritual father that God uses in your life repeatedly, should be respected and revered as the spiritual father who is your teacher, your mentor, your prophet or your leader. Although a spiritual father gives you the fatherly example, the fatherly advice and the fatherly wisdom, it does not mean that he is your spiritual father. He still should be respected for the father he is. Just because he's a spiritual father to someone, doesn't mean he is your spiritual father.

21. Spiritual fathers are more than likely to be a teacher to *many* and a father to *few* (I Corinthians 4:15).

22. There is no spiritual gifting, anointing, ability, talent or endowment that can substitute life experience. Humble yourself beneath the wings of the mature and the wise, which have lived longer than you have, and have done what you're trying to do.

23. If done properly, the counselor will be counseled as he counsels, and his conceitedness will diminish in every session.

24. The methodology we use to rehabilitate, inspire, and instruct shouldn't be void of wisdom, and must not be void of love. In our effort to get folk right, sometimes we forget the greater responsibility is to treat folk right.

25. If you're not obediently submitted to delegated or appointed authority, you aren't truly obediently submitted to the authority.

What Are You Thinking Now?

_____
_____
_____
_____
_____
_____
_____
_____
_____
_____
_____
_____
_____
_____
_____
_____
_____
_____
_____
_____
_____
_____
_____
_____
_____
_____
_____
_____
_____

For other books, teachings, and deliberations
from Dr. Larry D. Reid visit
http://www.sbmwinc.org

CPSIA information can be obtained
at www.ICGtesting.com
Printed in the USA
BVHW031130051121
620679BV00012B/230